1 MONTH OF
FREE
READING

at
www.ForgottenBooks.com

By purchasing this book you are eligible for one month membership to ForgottenBooks.com, giving you unlimited access to our entire collection of over 1,000,000 titles via our web site and mobile apps.

To claim your free month visit:
www.forgottenbooks.com/free584483

ISBN 978-0-484-16053-7
PIBN 10584483

Published by

GEE & CO., 34 Moorgate Street, LONDON, E.C.

ACCOUNTANT, THE (Established 1874). A weekly news-
paper. Price 6d. Subscription:—24s. per ann., post free U.K. Foreign, 26s.
Issued Weekly, in time for Friday evening's mail. *The Accountant* is the recognised
organ of Chartered Accountants and Accountancy throughout the world. It contains
Original Articles, Correspondence, Lectures and Debates on Bookkeeping (with
specimens of Accounts), Auditing, Liquidations, Bankruptcies, as well as Reports
of all Decisions as to Administration Cases, Arbitrations, Winding-up of Joint Stock
Companies, Liquidations, the Bankruptcy Act, Mercantile Law, and Partnerships, of
interest to Accountants; and is generally a complete Record of all Matters of Interest
to the Profession.

ACCOUNTANTS' JOURNAL. A monthly newspaper.
Price 9d., or 7s. 6d. per annum, post free U.K. Foreign 8s. 6d.
The general contents of the paper are designed more especially to meet the require-
ments of Accountant Students, though the practitioner is by no means overlooked. A
concise summary of the effect of all Important Legal Decisions appears in each number.
At least one original Article appears in each issue dealing with some matter
of interest to the Profession. The Lectures delivered to the various Students'
Societies are also reproduced. The Volume commences in May each year.
*Vols. I. to XII., Bound Half-Calf, Gold Lettered, Price 7s. 6d. net each, or 72/- for the
set of twelve; XIII. to XXIII., 8s. 6d. net each.*

ACCOUNTANTS' LIBRARY, THE. Under the above
heading a series of handbooks upon systems of Bookkeeping suitable for all
classes of undertakings is being issued. The books are published at a uniform
price of 3s. 6d. net, with the exception of a few "Double Numbers," for which the
price is 5s. To Subscribers these are published at the special rate of 2s. 6d. per
volume (3s. 9d. per "Double" volume). Subscriptions can still be received at this
reduced rate by those desirous of obtaining the whole Series. Subscribers who
may not wish to acquire the whole of the back volumes may, however, commence
their Subscription with Vol. XXI. A list of Volumes already published, and
Subscription Order Form, will be supplied post free on application.

ACCOUNTANT'S ASSISTANT, THE. 160 pages. Price
6s. net. By THOMAS BECKETT. This Work is an Index to the Accountancy
Lectures and Leading Articles printed in *The Accountant, The Accountants'
Journal*, The Transactions of the Various Students' Societies, and other
Periodicals from 1870-1900.

ACCOUNTANTS' (CHARTERED) CHARGES. (Third
Revised and Enlarged Edition.) Price 10s. 6d. net. By FRAS. W. PIXLEY, F.C.A.,
Barrister-at-Law.
One of the great wants of Members of the Profession is a Standard work of the Charges
of Chartered Accountants, to which they can refer their clients, when asked either to quote
a fee for future services or to support an account of Charges already rendered. This
work contains the Scale of Charges which prevails amongst the leading practising *London
Chartered Accountants* for *Auditing*, making *Investigations*, &c.—The *Charges of
Liquidators.*—The *Charges of Special Managers and Trustees in Bankruptcy, Receivers
in Chancery*, &c.—The *Charges for Assisting Debtors and Directors of Companies in
Liquidation* in the preparation of the *Statement of Affairs.*—The *Charges of Arbitrators,
Witnesses*, &c.

ACCOUNTANTS' DIARIES (Yearly), ruled, &c. Prices from
1s. 6d. to 10s.—Editions Nos. 1, 2, 3 and 3A are specially Ruled and Headed according to the Pattern approved by most practising Accountants. All Editions except
the 1s. 6d. contain a Directory of Accountants and much useful information.

ACCOUNTANT'S AND BOOKKEEPER'S VADE-MECUM. Price
7s. 6d. net. By G. E. STUART WHATLEY, Accountant (Exam. Inst. C.A.).
The Work consists of a *Series of short and Concise Articles* upon *Capital and
Revenue Expenditure, Revenue Accounts, Deficiency Accounts, Depreciation, Reserve
and Sinking Funds, Adjustment of Partnership Accounts, Joint Stock Companies'
Accounts, Tabular Bookkeeping, Hotel and Theatre Accounts*, and other matters not
generally dealt with in existing *Works on Bookkeeping*, together with useful *Forms* and
Directions.

CATALOGUE OF BOOKS FREE.

[605.2M.3.08.]

ACCOUNTANTS' MANUAL, published biennially, with Index. Subscription 3s. 6d. per annum. Vols. I., II., III., IV., V., VI., VII., VIII., IX., and X., now ready, price 12s. 6d. each (except Vol. III., 10s. 6d.) or £5 the set. Also issued in parts every June and December, price 2s. 6d. each.

The only complete and full set of Answers to the Questions set at the Institute of Chartered Accountants' Examinations, dating from December 1884. These Answers are designed to give the fullest and most reliable information on each question asked, and are compiled with a view to lasting reference.

ACCOUNTANT'S COMPENDIUM, THE. Third Edition in the Press. A complete Lexicon for Accountants. By SIDNEY STANLEY DAWSON, F.C.A., F.C.I.S.. F.S.S.

ADVANCED ACCOUNTING. Third Edition. Revised and Enlarged. Price 21s. net. By LAWRENCE R. DICKSEE, M.Com., F.C.A., Professor of Accounting at the University of Birmingham (Author of "Auditing," "Bookkeeping for Accountant Students," &c.)

This work will be found of the greatest value to Candidates for the Final Examination of the Institute, and to all serious Students of Accounts. In addition to an exhaustive treatment of the subject from an Accountant's point of view, an Appendix is included, which has been written by J. E. G. DE MONTMORENCY, B.A., LL.B. (Cantab), of the Middle Temple, Barrister-at-Law, dealing with the law relating to accounts, and the requirements of the Courts and of lawyers in connection therewith.

ANTE-AUDIT. Price 1s. each net; 5s. 6d. ½-dozen copies; 10s. 1 dozen copies. Being the Auditor's Instructions to his Client's Book-keeping Staff. Issued in connection with the series of AUDIT NOTE-BOOKS Nos. 1, 2, and 3.

AUDIT NOTE-BOOK. Nos. I. & II., Price 6d. (net) each, 5s. per dozen. 40/- per hundred. Issued in two Series, viz.:—
No. 1—Suitable for a Monthly Audit.
No. 2—Suitable for a Quarterly or Half-yearly Audit. Name and address printed on Covers free on orders of 100 or more copies.

AUDIT NOTE-BOOK No. 3. New and Enlarged Edition. (For Important Audits.) 100 pages, Foolscap 4to. Price 2s. per copy, 20s. per dozen, or 70s. for 50 copies, and £5 10s. for 100 copies. Name and address printed on cover if 50 or more copies are ordered.

AUDITING. A Practical Manual for Auditors. Seventh Edition. Price 21s. net. By LAWRENCE R. DICKSEE, M.Com., F.C.A.

A New and Enlarged Edition of this Standard Work. The text has been thoroughly revised, in part re-written, and brought entirely up to date. Special attention has been devoted to the Accounts of Local Authorities and their Audit, Depreciation, Sinking Funds, &c.

AUDITS. 160 pages. Price 5s. net. By ARTHUR E. CUTFORTH, A.C.A. This little work has been compiled with two main objects. It is an attempt to lay down, within the limits of a book of moderate size, the main duties of Auditors, and the principles affecting their work, and regard has also been had to the needs and requirements of Students for Examinations, in the choice and treatment of the subjects dealt with.

BANKRUPTCY. Second and enlarged Edition. Price 7s. 6d. net. By T. M. STEVENS, D.C.L., Barrister-at-Law.

This work, whilst treating the subject from a legal point of view, will still be *of use mainly to Chartered Accountants* and others. The general outlines of the subject, *i.e., the text of the Acts, as explained by leading cases, is what is wanted, and what this work has endeavoured to give.*

BANKRUPTCY TRUSTEE'S ESTATE BOOK, THE. Second Edition. Price 4s. net.

Compiled by LAWRENCE R. DICKSEE, M.Com., F.C.A. Author of "Auditing," &c. This Book contains the whole of the information likely to be required by Trustees in Bankruptcy in such a form that in conjunction with the "Record Book" it provides a complete statement of all the facts relating to any particular estate, entirely doing away with the necessity for memorandum and loose sheets, which are so frequently lost.

BOOKKEEPING EXERCISES for Accountant Students. Demy 8vo, about 96 pages. Price 3s. 6d. By LAWRENCE R. DICKSEE, M.Com., F.C.A., Author of "Auditing," "Bookkeeping for Accountant Students," "Bookkeeping for Company Secretaries," &c.

SPECIAL TERMS FOR PUBLISHING AUTHORS' WORKS

BOOKKEEPING FOR ACCOUNTANT STUDENTS.

Fifth Edition. Complete, with Index, 10s. 6d. net. By LAWRENCE R. DICKSEE, M.Com., F.C.A. (of the firm of Sellars, Dicksee & Co.)

Contains a full and complete explanation of the *Theory of Double Entry*, and is supplemented by copious *Exercises* and *Questions* that combine to make it a work of the highest educational value.

BOOKKEEPING FOR COMPANY SECRETARIES.

Fourth Edition. Price 5s. net. By LAWRENCE R. DICKSEE. M.Com., F.C.A.

This Work deals very fully with those questions in relation to Bookkeeping, a knowledge of which is essential upon the part of every Company Secretary.

BOOT AND SHOE COSTINGS AND PERIODICAL MANU-FACTURING, TRADING, AND FINANCIAL STATEMENTS.

By LAWRANCE C. HEADLY, Chartered Accountant. Price 2s. 9d. net, post free.

. The first part describes a simple and practical system for checking costs in detail, and ascertaining the results of manufacturing, the profits and losses in connection with the working up and consumption of materials and in connection with wages— the items of prime cost. It shows how the Factory Accounts are so designed that the results obtained by them can be corroborated by the audited accounts.

The second part deals with Trading, and the expenses of carrying on the business, and gives examples of periodical statements by means of which full information on every detail can be obtained.

BREWERS' ACCOUNTS. By H. LANHAM, A.C.A.

200 pages. Price 10s. 6d. net. This Work deals very fully with the important questions of Bottled Beer Accounts, Stock Books, and the treatment in the books of payments under the "Compensation Act," thus making it the most complete and up-to-date Book published on these subjects.

COMPANY-SECRETARY, THE. Sixth Edition. Price

25s. net. (Foolscap folio.) By W. H. FOX, Chartered Accountant. Containing a Full Description of the Duties of the Company-Secretary, together with an APPENDIX of FORMS and PRECEDENTS.

COMPARATIVE DEPRECIATION TABLES. Price

1s. net. By LAWRENCE R. DICKSEE, M.Com., F.C.A.

Containing a full set of Tables, showing the practical effect of providing for depreciation on the Fixed Instalment and the Fixed Percentage methods, and discussing their respective advantages.

COST ACCOUNTS. The following Volumes on COST

ACCOUNTS have been issued in "THE ACCOUNTANTS' LIBRARY" series:— MULTIPLE COST ACCOUNTS, by H. STANLEY GARRY. Price 3s. 6d. net, TERMINAL COST ACCOUNTS, by A. G. NISBET. Price 3s. 6d. net, SINGLE COST ACCOUNTS, by G. A. MITCHELL. Price 5s. net. PROCESS COST ACCOUNTS, by STANLEY GARRY. Price 5s. net.

COST ACCOUNTS: AN EXPLANATION OF PRINCIPLES AND A GUIDE TO PRACTICE Price 5s. net. By L. WHITTEM

HAWKINS, Chartered Accountant.

Contains an explanation of the general principles governing the ascertainment of manufacturing cost, with full and lucid instructions for the practical application of those principles, and is illustrated by an Explanatory Diagram, a Set of Forms, and a Worked Example.

COST ACCOUNTS OF AN ENGINEER AND IRON-FOUNDER, THE. Price 2s. 6d. net. By J. W. BEST,

F.C.A. The first portion deals with the Engineering and the second with the Foundry Department, and numerous forms of books and accounts are given and explained.

DEEDS OF ARRANGEMENT. By D. P. DAVIES,

F.S.A.A. Price 8s. net. 220 pages. A Practical Manual for the Use of Trustees. The fact that no book exists dealing with Deeds of Assignment from an administrative point of view has led the Author to embody here the results of nearly twenty years' active insolvency experience. Special attention has been given to the requirements of Trustees, and all points, legal and otherwise, likely to arise in the administration of an estate are dealt with. Where cases are reported in *The Accountant* Law Reports, special reference is made thereto, for the convenience of Accountants.

BOOT & SHOE COSTINGS

BY

LAWRANCE C. HEADLY, A.CA.

BOOT & SHOE COSTINGS

BY

LAWRANCE C. HEADLY, A.C.A.

———————

LONDON :

GEE & CO., Printers and Publishers, 34 Moorgate Street, E.C.

—

1908.

INTRODUCTION.

THE system described in the following pages is not the theory of a doctrinaire, but a practical system in actual operation. By its means can be ascertained, daily, the profits and losses on the cutting up of materials; weekly, the profits and losses on wages and grinderies and the manufacturing gross profit; also the profits and losses on bottom stuff at certain periods, and on each lot of leather purchased, whether for uppers or bottoms, as it is consumed. It shows how the factory accounts dealing with manufacturing and consumption of materials can be designed to fit in with the Trading and Profit and Loss Accounts, and the results of the one checked and corroborated by the results of the other. It may be protested that, for practical purposes, it is over-elaborate—that grinderies, for instance, are a small matter and afford little scope for losses, to regard it from no other point of view. It may be so and it may not. The more accurate information there is available the better, and, if it is considered desirable to have it, the machinery for supplying it is described. But the system is elastic. It can be commenced in a small way to embrace, to start with, the upper stuff, bottom stuff, wages, manufacturing profit, and the grindery for a particular room, and extended as its advantages become apparent.

The working conditions of factories, of course, vary, and there may be details of the system inapplicable to a particular case, but these would only require adapting and modifying to suit the circumstances.

The second part treats of accounts dealing with the financial situation, and Sales, Purchases, Wages, and Expenses, and other cognate matters. It shows how by simple bookkeeping devices these accounts can be prepared periodically with very little trouble.

It is the earnest wish of most manufacturers to know, from day to day, "what they are doing." A large proportion only know results when, at the end of the financial period, they are in possession of periodical accounts, which, in most cases, disclose facts the reverse of expectations which are not unusually sanguine.

And as a growing business passes that stage in its evolution when it becomes necessary, by reason of its size, to delegate authority and responsibility to managers of departments into which it is essential to divide it, it is more than ever important that an adequate system should be organised for providing, automatically as it were, reliable statistics and information as to how these departments are working.

It is possible then for, to use Professor Marshall's words, the head of a large business to reserve all his strength for the broadest and most fundamental problems of his trade : he must indeed assure himself that his managers, clerks, and foremen are the right men for their work ; but beyond that he need not trouble himself much about details. He can keep his mind fresh and clear for thinking out the most difficult and vital problems of his business ; for studying the broader movements of the markets, the yet undeveloped results of current events at home and abroad ; and for contriving how to improve the organisation of the internal and external relations of his business.

18 Friar Lane,

Leicester,

25th September 1907.

BOOT AND SHOE COSTINGS.

PART I.

It is unnecessary to descant on the value of reliable information as to the costs of manufacture, finances, the general course of trade, together with the expenses incurred, especially in cases of large aggregations of capital working on small margins of profit. The more successful a business the more highly organised and efficient the systems; they are some of the chief causes of the success. The story of the bungs in the history of the Standard Oil Trust gives some idea of the effective organisation employed by the largest commercial undertaking in the world.

In most businesses of any magnitude there are usually some kinds of systems for obtaining the necessary information, varying, however, in their efficiency. More often than not perhaps they are unreliable, and it is seldom that any of those for checking the prime costs of raw material and wages are so designed that the cumulative results obtained from them can be corroborated in detail by the figures of the audited accounts.

The example set out in the pages immediately following illustrates such a system applied to a boot factory.

It is submitted that in designing a system for checking prime costs there are, besides others, six cardinal principles to be observed : —

(1) That the expense of it does not exceed a sum which can justifiably be incurred.

(2) That it does not impede or interfere with the working of the factory or workshop.

(3) That it is simple.

(4) That it is automatic and its results are available, daily, weekly, monthly, as the work proceeds, when they are of service and can be utilised.

(5) That it is reliable, and its results are corroborated by the audited accounts at stated periods.

(6) That it should be a uniform system applicable throughout.

It must be borne in mind also that it is designed particularly for the purpose of discovering mistakes made inadvertently, and not wilful attempts on the part of dishonest workpeople to cheat and defraud their employers. It will, no doubt, serve the latter purpose; but that is not its primary object, and to provide for it would perhaps make the scheme hopelessly complicated and unworkable.

To observe the first and second of these principles it will be generally admitted that any system designed to check all the items constituting the prime cost of any article or number of similar articles with scientific precision is impossible, and that therefore the main points to be kept in view are:—

(1) A checking in detail of the costings of raw material, which affords scope for losses on account of its variability in the way of quality, substance, texture, and so forth as it is worked up.

(2) A checking of the costings of productive wages day by day, week by week, month by month, and in particular on particular orders, whether for customers or for stock.

(3) A checking of the costings, in the bulk and at certain periods, of these raw materials, the quantity or weight of which for any particular article can be ascertained almost accurately. For instance, in a boot having a certain number of eyelet holes, these are, of course, counted, a proportion allowed in addition for waste, the cost of the total of these ascertained, which is the sum put down for the cost of eyelets in the costing.

So far as I know, the actual business of costing a boot does not materially differ from the costing of most other manufactured articles. The cost is entered up on a page of the Costing Book, specially designed, and providing the requisite printed headings for the cost of the various materials and labour operations, each item of cost having first been obtained from samples put through the factory to ascertain the facts required, and from other information obtained in the course of experience and carefully recorded. Form 1 is a specimen costing of a dozen pairs of lady's boots. To obtain the selling price a certain percentage is added.

In checking the costings of the labour operations, matters are much simplified, because they can be classified, each class or series of operations by which the manufacture is advanced a stage being executed in one room, or part of a room, and the workpeople engaged on that particular kind of labour kept separate. There are in all five broad distinct classes of operations, and therefore five departments of productive labour : —

(1) Clicking or cutting the upper part of the article from skins and materials, executed in the Clicking Room. (There are other subsidiary operations executed in this room—such as " skiving," thinning the edge of the leather so that it will be less bulky when turned in, and " turning in "—but these operations are classified with the chief operation of clicking.) The chief operations in the other departments may have also subsidiary operations ; in each case these are included in the chief operation.

Form 1.—

No. : 4,061
Class : Seconds Glacé
Bottom No. : B 34
Fitting : D 4
Make : M S.
Finish : 47
Heel : 8
Cap No. : 50
Topband No. : 16
Lining : 2
Stiffner : 5
Description : Lady's Black Glacé Kid Lace Boot, Self Straight Cap, Vamp, Cap and Quarters turned in, Top Bagged Deep, Ribbon Top Band, Best White Lining, Persian Facing, Celluloid Eyelets, no facing row, Lined Tongue, Leather Sock

	Material	Wages	Total
	£ s d	£ s d	£ s d
UPPERS—			
Legs, 17/-			
Vamp, 10/-			
Cap, 1/6	1 8 6		
Lining	0 1 6		
Facing	0 1 0		
Top Band	0 2 0		
Tongues	0 0 9	..	1 13 9
	1 13 9		
Clicking	..	0 2 6	0 2 6
			1 16 3
Eyelets	0 0 9½		
Eyeletting	..	0 0 2½	
Machining	..	0 3 3	
Do. Grindery	0 0 3	..	
	1 14 9½	0 5 11½	0 4 6
BOTTOMS, &c.—			
Bottoms, 7/6, 2/-, 1/8, 4d.	0 11 6		
Socks	0 1 3		
Heels	0 4 2		
Heeling	..	0 0 4	
			0 17 3
Cutting	..	0 1 3	
Lasting	..	0 3 9	
Do. Grindery	0 0 7		
Finishing	..	0 3 9	
Do. Grindery	0 0 4		
Fitting up	..	0 0 3	
Royalty	0 0 3		
Sewing and Cord	0 0 5		
Boxes	0 1 0		
Packing and Treeing	..	0 0 6	
			0 2 7
			0 9 6
Cost of Material and Wages	£2 14 3½	£0 15 9½	£3 10 1
Management per Cent., &c.			

(2) Machining the component parts of these uppers together in the Machine Room—such as the vamp to the golosh, linings and tongues in their appropriate position, and so on.

(3) Lasting or attaching by sewing or rivetting in the Lasting Room the uppers to the sole, which is obtained from the Press Room—this room is described further on—and attaching the heel.

(4) Finishing the sole and heel in the Finishing Room ; giving them a pleasing shape and appearance. They come in a rough unsightly state from the Lasting Room.

(5) Cutting up the sole leather or bottom stuff, executed in the Press Room, in which room also the uppers are fitted with the requisite bottoms as they come from the Machine Room. Soles are costed by weight per dozen pairs, and the selection is done by "fitters up," who from long experience can judge the weight by eye and hand to a nicety.

Besides these rooms there is a Skin Room, in which the stock of skins and materials for uppers are kept contiguous, if possible, to the Clicking Room, and, of course, there are in some convenient part Stock Rooms and Packing Rooms.

The rooms are disposed so that, as each class of operations is completed, the article has as small a distance to travel as possible to reach the room where the next class is performed.

Turning to the specimen costing, the first item is self-explanatory—the number of the boot. These numbers run consecutively. Seconds glacé means the second quality in the glacé kid. With the exception of the D4 against last and fitting, the numbers against each of the other items represent the kind or variety of the materials or treatment which is to be utilised or applied to this particular boot. Each Department has its own appropriate list, showing under corresponding numbers the requisite particulars. The D4 against "Last and Fitting" indicate the last of a particular fitting to be used. D Last 4 Fitting would be an accurate way of describing it. There are a variety of lasts, of course, all of different shapes, each variety being in eight sizes or lengths, and each size having different fittings or measurements round the foot at the joint of the big toe. The stiffner is the stiff piece of material fitted in the upper round the back of the heel to keep that part of the upper stiff and upright.

The description of the boot is fairly simple and straight-forward. A self cap is a cap made of the same material as the vamp; the Persian facing is the narrow strip of Persian leather running down inside on both sides of the opening to strengthen the part where the eyelets are inserted; the top bagged deep is a technical term for expressing a certain way of joining the leather and lining inside at the top of the leg; a facing row is a row of machining which is sometimes worked in down the boot outside each of the rows of eyelets as an ornament. This particular boot has none; the fact, however, has to be noted to avoid mistakes.

As regards the cost, the items for material and labour are entered in separate columns. The cost is per dozen pairs, and the size selected for costing is No. 5, this being the average size. The total cost on leaving the Clicking Room is £1 16s. 3d.; the cost of additional material and wages in the Machine Room is 4s. 6d., making £2 0s. 9d., and the further cost of bottoms, heels, socks, cord, boxes, the grindery in the Lasting and Finishing Rooms, with the labour operations of fitting up the uppers with the requisite bottoms, lasting (sewing or rivetting) the bottoms to the uppers, packing and treeing (treeing being the operation of finishing the uppers on a treeing machine by a treatment to give the surface a higher finish) royalty in respect of machines on lease, and for which royalties have to be paid. The further cost of all these items amounts to £1 9s. 4d., making a total of £3 10s. 1d. The printed heading of Management per cent., &c., is provided for an item of cost in connection with such matters as wages of foremen, liftman, superintendent of stores, looker up of orders. It can be either a percentage or a rate per number of articles manufactured per week.

With the exception of the items of grindery, the details of the cost are self-explanatory. Grindery is the generic term used to denote a quantity of small articles and preparations. The grindery of the Machine Room includes cotton, thread, silk, needles, and so on; of the Lasting Room, lasting tacks, rivets, &c.; of the Finishing Room, stains and inks for colouring the bottoms, knives, sandpaper, brushes, &c.

The figures against the bottom are the cost in order of the outsole, insole, stiffner, puffs, shanking, and bottom filling.

Puffs are shaped pieces of cardboard to insert in the toe of the boot and maintain its shape; shanking is a strip of leather along the bottom to keep rigid the waist—that portion of the sole between the heel and wider part trodden on—and bottom filling is leather inserted in the space made vacant by the edges of the upper being turned over the insole.

Sewing is the operation of lasting by sewing the upper to the insole, and the cord is the material used for that purpose.

In order to ascertain the first item of cost—Legs, Vamp, and Cap, 28s. 6d.—a certain number of skins are cut up in the Clicking Room, the facts recorded on sheets similar to Form 2, which are sent down to the costing clerk. Now skins of the same kind vary in substance and quality, and clickers vary in their technical skill and care, so that in order to obtain an average cost it will be necessary to have more than one skin cut up—it may be necessary to have a dozen—it may be necessary to have six dozen—the number depends upon the variableness of the skins.

Form 2.—

Clicker *Jones* .... Date out .... In .... Material *Glace Kid*

		£ s d				£ s d
Feet .. 354¾	8½d	12 11 3	82	4,061—complete ..	28/6	9 14 9
			18	Stock Boot Legs..	13/6	1 0 3
			54	,, Vamps ..	5/6	1 4 9
			32	,, Quarters ..	5/-	0 13 4
Weight 32 0						
				10 lbs 10 oz. Offal	6d.	0 5 3½
Profit ..		0 7 1½				
		£12 18 4½				£12 18 4½

Weight ..	32 0		Weight—Returns			
			Cut Stuff ..	19 0		
			Offal	10 10		
			Scraps.. ..	2 6		
	32 (			32 0		

This Costing Sheet shows on the debit the number of feet which the skins measure as given out from the Skin Room to the clicker, and the price of same per foot. On the credit is shown what has been obtained from these skins. The first item consists of 82 pairs of legs, vamps, and caps, for the boot No. 4,061 as costed. No more could be obtained, and the remainder of the skins were cut up into stock boot legs, vamps, and quarters, which will be utilised in due time for the boots for which they are appropriate, which may be what are called running in lines—boots designed especially for their utilisation.

The next item is 10lbs. 10oz. of offal, which consists of the smaller pieces of leather, to be returned to the Skin Room, and which will be used in due time for such purposes as tongues, facings, back straps, and so on. Taking the various articles obtained from the leather given out, and pricing these out at the various figures in the different costings, and pricing the offal at its value for the use as above stated, we have a credit figure of £12 18s. 4½d., against a debit of £12 11s. 3d., which shows a profit of 7s. 1½d. Below these is given a Profit and Loss Account of the weights. On the debit is shown the weight of the skins given out, amounting to 32lbs; on the credit side is shown the weight of the articles cut. The articles cut weigh 19 lbs., the offal 10 lbs. 10 oz., leaving as scrap 2 lbs. 6 oz. The scrap is worthless, but the object of showing these details is to ascertain the amount of scrap, because, of course, if the scrap is excessive the skins are not being cut up most advantageously. As instancing the variability of the skins, Form 3 is a Costing Sheet of a parcel of the same lot of skins cut up at a loss. The costs of the other materials, excluding grindery, are obtained in a similar manner. The lining and top-band being cut from materials which do not vary in substance and quality like skins, the cutting up of a certain length will provide the requisite information.

Form 3.—

Clicker_____ *Brown*_____ Date out_____ In_____ Material _Glace Kid_

		£ s d				£ s d
Feet .. 156¼	8½d	5 10 8	34	4,061—complete..	28/6	4 0 9
			12½	Vamps	6/-	0 6 3
			30	Stock Backs ..	5/-	0 12 6
				5 lbs. Offal	6d.	0 2 6
Weight 14 4						
						5 2 0
				Loss		0 8 8
		£5 10 8				£5 10 8

Weight .. 14 4		Weight—Returns ..	0 4
		Cut Stuff ..	8 2
		Offal	5 0
		Scraps ..	0 14
	14 4		14 4

The labour operations being paid in all departments by time as well as by piece-work, an estimate will have to be made to cover the cost of hands on the manufacturer's own time, which will be based on the facts ascertained from experience.

As regards the Bottoms, Form 4 is a Costing Sheet of the cutting up of a parcel of bottom leather. The insoles, 2s., used in the boot 4,061 are made from this leather, the outsoles being obtained from another kind of leather. Middles or middle soles are used to strengthen light outsoles by being attached to them, so giving them the requisite weight and substance. Top-pieces, seat lifts, and lifts are used for heels only, top-pieces, being the best piece of leather, are used for the top of the heel, which gets most wear. Seat lifts are the pieces at the bottom of the heel next the shoe, and the lifts are used for the body of the heel. Half-lifting and scraps are deemed worthless.

Form 4.—

ROBINSON.

1907 June 4	English Bellies— c. qrs. lbs. 4 0 5 453 lbs. 1/- ..	£ s d			lbs. oz.	doz.		£ s d
		22 13 0	60·9	Ladies'best Insoles ..	99 12	„	2/6	7 11 10
			26·3	Com. canvas Outsoles..	65 0	„	3/6	4 11 10½
			35·0	2nd Insoles	53 12	„	2/-	3 10 0
			27·6	Middles ..	29 4	lb.	10d.	1 4 4
			16·0	Stiffners ..	12 6	doz.	1/6	1 4 0
				Top-pieces ..	32 0	lb.	1/-	1 12 0
				Seat Lifts ..	7 12	„	8d.	0 5 2
				Lifts	65 0	„	8d.	2 3 4
				½-Lifting ..	28 0			
				Scraps.. ..	54 8			
					447 6			22 2 6½
				Loss				0 10 5½
		£22 13 0						£22 13 0

As regards the Heels, they are either bought or made. If made, the wages are kept separate and the material is costed per pound, and as the moulds can only hold a certain quantity the ascertainment of the cost presents no particular difficulty.

Form 5.

Date *May 16th, 1907.*
When Wanted *July 1st.*
No. of Boot *4061.*
Description *Glace Lace.*

D 4

House No. 26.
Order No. 3416.
Serial No. 2407.

Stock Room.
Serial No. 2407.

Finishing Room.
36 Pairs 4061.
Serial No. 2407.

Rivetting Room.
36 Pairs 4061.
Serial No. 2407.

Fitting Up Room.
36 Pairs 4061.
Serial No. 297.

Machine Room.
36 Pairs 4061.
Serial No. 297.

36 Pairs 4061.
Serial No. 297.

This Sheet must not leave any Department until the work is complete.

PAIRS	2	3	4	5	6	7	8	9	10	11	12	13	1	Clicker
36		6	9	12	6	3								
		Bottom			*B* 34									
		Finish.			47									

Clicking Room	Machine Room	Fitting up Room	Rivetting Room	Finishing Room	Stock Room
Date	Date	Date	Date	Date	Date

Checked by

B

As regards the item Sewing and Cord, the operation of sewing is paid for per dozen pairs; and the quantity of cord used can, of course, be easily ascertained.

The costing of the boot being completed, the description, together with the particulars enumerated against the illustration, are copied into a book under the charge of the foreman of the Clicking Room. On an order being received it is entered in the Order Book under a consecutive number, known as the Order number, and each half-gross, or quantity less than half-a-gross, is given also a consecutive number, known as a Serial number. A ticket is made out (Form 5) for the number of pairs in respect of each serial number and sent to the Clicking Room, where small tickets (Form 6) are made out to be attached to each dozen.

The skins are then given out, the work in the Clicking Room is performed, the coupon marked " Clicking Room " on the large ticket (Form 5) is dated and detached, the edge being perforated, and placed in a box provided for the purpose. The goods, with the large ticket attached to one of the lots of dozen bundles, are handed on to the Machine Room. When they are ready to leave that room the appropriate coupon is removed and preserved, the same process being followed as the goods pass from room to room.

Every morning these boxes containing the coupons are brought down from each room to the Counting House, where they are entered up in the Goods in Process Book (Form 7), which affords valuable information as to the process of manufacture of each order and its position in the factory. They are then handed on to the costing clerk who, with these coupons and the Costing Sheets sent down from the Clicking Room and the details of cost in the Costing Book, works out the Profit and Loss Accounts for materials and wages for each department.

Form 6 (continued). (Reverse side).

O

Seconds Glace Bals.; self straight cap.

Vamp cap and quarters turned in; top bagged deep.

No. 16 top-band; 50 cap.

Best white lined No. 2 Persian facing.

Celluloid eyelets; no facing row.

Lined tongue.

Form 6.—

O

Order No. 3,416

Ser. No. 2,407

2	3	4	5	6	7	8	9	10	11	12	13	1
	6	9	12	6	3							

Boot No. 4,061

Ake   Ms

Bottom No. B 34

Last   D—4

Heel   8

Fish   47

Sock   Leather

Form 7.—

GOODS IN PROCESS BOOK.

Serial No.	Order No.	Boot No.	Clicking Room		Mach-ine Room	Fitting Up	Lasting Room	Finish-ing Room	Stock Room
			In	Out	Out	Out	Out	Out	Out
			(Date)	(Date)	(Date)	(Date)	(Date)	(Date)	(Date)

No skin is cut up without a Costing Sheet similar to Form 2 being made out. These Costing Sheets are sent from the Clicking Room, priced out, and the results recorded in a book called "Record of Cuttings" (Form 8). It provides on the debit side columns for the date, the distinguishing number of the Costing Sheet, the lot number and the kind of leather, the value of the leather given out; and on the credit side, the number of the boot for which it has been used, the amount on the credit side of the Costing Sheet comprising the value of articles obtained at the price in the Costing Book without and with the offal returned to the Skin Room, the profit, and the loss. The profits and losses are summarised each week at the bottom of the sheet. At the end of each month these summaries are again summarised as shown in Form 9.

Form 8.—

Date	Number of Costing Sheet	Lot No. and Kind of Leather	Net value of Material given out			Boot No.	Cost of Boot without Offal			Cost of Boot with Offal			Profit			Loss		
			£	s	d		£	s	d	£	s	d	£	s	d	£	s	d
June	1	8 Black Glace Kid	5	18	2	5	6	1	10	6	5	10	0	7	8			
,,	,,	3 Mock Kid	1	2	10	8	1	5	6	1	6	4	0	3	6	0	10	1
,,	,,	2 Box Calf	3	4	5	300	2	13	4	2	14	4			6	0	3	6
,,	,,	1 Chrome Sheep	1	18	6	401	1	14	0	1	14	6	0	..	2			
,,	,,	5 Tan Gue Kid	2	5	6	415	2	6	10	2	8	0			6	0	1	2
,,	,,	12 Tan Kip Bellies	0	18	6	2	0	17	0	0	17	6	0	..	1			
,,	,,	15 Blk Tace Kid	1	17	6	7	1	17	4	1	18	6	0	..	6			
,,	,,	6 Chrome Sheep	6	18	6	15	6	0	6	6	3	6			0	0	15	0
,,	,,	17 Box Calf	4	3	10	52	4	13	6	4	16	0	0	13	..			
,,	,,	40 Tan Glace Kid	8	2	6	39	8	18	0	9	0	6	0	18	..			
,,	,,	43 Blk Tace Kid	9	10	0	78	8	0	0	8	19	6			..	0	10	6
			£45	19	3		£44	7	4	£46	5	2	£2	6	2	£2	0	3

SUMMARY OF EACH PAGE:—

	Lot No. and Kind of Leather													Profit			Loss		
														£	s	d	£	s	d
	Black Glace Kid													0	9	2	0	10	6
	Mock Kid													0	3	6	0	10	1
	Box Calf													0	13	0	0	18	6
	Chrome Sheep													1	0	6	0	1	2
	Tan Glace Kid																		
	,, Kip Bellies													£2	6	2	£2	0	3

Form 9.

WEEKLY PROFIT AND LOSS ON CUTTING OF MATERIALS,
June 18th to 23rd 1906.

	Profit	Loss	Net Profit	Net Loss
	£ s d	£ s d	£ s d	£ s d
Black Glace Kid ..	6 11 6	5 10 11		
Mock Kid ..	0 10 0	0 2 6		
Box Calf ..	3 4 6	2 19 2		
Chrome Sheep ..	0 1 0	1 15 0		
Tan Glace Kid ..	2 17 6	0 15 1		
Tan Kip Bellies..	0 18 6	0 2 0		
Willow Calf ..	..	1 13 6		
Chrome Lambs ..		0 15 0		
Black Roans ..	0 7 11	..		
Glace Offal.. ..	0 1 6			
Box Hide		0 5 6		
Glove Hide ..	3 2 6	2 17 0		
Tan Hide Bellies ..	..	0 17 6		
	£17 14 11	£17 13 2	£0 1 9	

This book therefore records the actual profit or loss in detail on all the skins cut up, but there is a further fact which it is essential should be ascertained—namely, the result in the bulk of the cutting up of each lot of skins purchased. Each lot of skins purchased is given a lot number, which runs consecutively. As soon as the lot has been passed into stock this number is communicated to the Costing Department with a description of the leather, and the invoice price is obtained. A book is kept on the debit and credit system, and an account is opened (Form 10) for each lot of leather, to which it is debited: particulars of the weight, number of feet, and price, being given. To each account is credited the consumption as shown by the Costing Sheets, from which the entries are made from time to time. This account will show the stock on hand, which should

Form 10.—   Lot No. 410. Seconds Glace.

1906 June 1	To 750 feet 70 lbs. ..	8½	£ s d 26 11 3	1906 June 1	By 101	lbs oz 32 0	£ s d 12 18 4½

be checked with the actual stock in the Skin Room occasionally, and also, when the whole of the lot is cut up, the resultant profit or loss.

As regards the bottom leather, an exactly similar system as that adopted with skins is followed. The sheets showing the cutting up are sent into the Costing Department. A book is kept containing accounts of each lot purchased, which are written up in a similar manner to the Lot Accounts for skins. The Costing Sheets are also entered up in a Record of Cuttings Book similar to the one used for skins, and weekly and monthly summaries of the profits and losses made.

As skins are only cut up for a particular boot, the amount for that portion of it made out of skins in the costing is checked at the time, and the result is immediately available, which is most important. Bottom leather is cut up to provide stock, so that a further system to check the amount in the Costing Book for the bottoms has to be designed.

On being cut, the bottom leather is handed on to the Fitting-up Department, ranged, of course, according to the weight per dozen pairs. As already explained, the fitting-up is done by weight, the hand and eye alone being relied on, and the danger is that a heavier and better quality bottom than that costed for may be fitted up. Moreover, the weight of the sole leather is artificially increased in the Press Room by immersion in water.

Unfortunately, the checking of the costings of bottoms cannot be done in detail as they are fitted up. The costings have to be checked in the bulk and at certain periods when stock is taken. A Profit and Loss Account is made out (Form 11), showing on the one hand the stock of bottom stuff at the commencement, the purchases of raw material of the same during the period, and the wages paid to the heelers; and, on the other, the value of the bottoms and heels fitted up at costing

Form II.—

BOTTOM STUFF PROFIT AND LOSS ACCOUNT from 1st January to 30th June 1906.

1906		£ s d	£ s d	£ s d
Jan. 1	To Stock:—			
	Raw Material ..	8,000 0 0		
	Do. Heeling Grindery ..	10 0 0		
			8,010 0 0	
	Cut Stuff ..£1,000 0 0			
	Heels .. 250 0 0			
			1,250 0 0	
June 30	„ Purchases ..		9,260 0 0	
	„ Heeling Wages ..		10,000 0 0	
			210 0 0	
			£19,470 0 0	

1906		£ s d	£ s d	£ s d
June 30	By Value of Bottoms fitted up as per Coupons ..			12,000 0 0
	„ Stock:—			
	Raw Material ..	6,300 0 0		
	Heeling Grindery ..	195 0 0		
			6,495 0 0	
	Cut Stuff ..£600 0 0			
	Heels.. .. 175 0 0			
			775 0 0	
				7,270 0 0
	„ Loss ..			200 0 0
				£19,470 0 0

price, and the stock of bottom stuff and heels at the end of the period. The bottoms and heels fitted up are obtained by means of the coupons sent down from the Fitting-up Department, and the value at which the bottoms and heels are taken is the amount of same in the Costing Book, which in boot No. 4,061 is 11s. 6d. and 4s. respectively.

In addition to this check in the bulk, surprise visits should be frequently paid to the Fitting-up Department, and the soles which have been put out to be lasted to the uppers taken out from their receptacles and weighed, the weights so ascertained being compared with the weights of the bottom specified for the particular boot.

With reference to the costings for Linings, Facings, Top-bands, Eyelets, and Tongues, the items of Legs, Vamps, and Caps are included, and the checking of the whole of these done in the bulk after stocktakings, a Manufacturing Profit and Loss Account being prepared on the same principles as those adopted for the bottom stuff. The purchases are obtained from the Invoice Book (Form 12), and the amount receivable for the period from the boots manufactured, from the Coupon Tickets. If desirable, the purchases in respect of these items can be analysed, and separate Profit and Loss Accounts prepared for skins and linings, facings, top-bands, and eyelets.

As regards the costings for Socks, Cord for sewing, and Boxes, these are also checked in the bulk after stocktakings in a similar way to that followed for the bottom stuff.

As regards Royalty, this should be checked in the bulk monthly. The monthly invoice for royalty gives the amount incurred, and the coupons from the Lasting Room give the necessary information for obtaining the amount receivable for the work performed on the royalty machines.

Form 12.—

INVOICE BOOK.

Date	Name	No. of Invoice	Ledger Folio	Amount			Skins and other Materials for Uppers			Bottom Stuff, Socks, Heels, and Grindery for Heels			Cord and Boxes			Royalty			Grinderies									Cases and Packing Materials			Plant Machinery			Lasts and Knives			Repairs to Plant and Machinery			Repairs to Lasts and Knives			Sundries
																				Machine Room			Lasting Room			Finishing Room																			[This column to be analysed at the end of each month.]
				£	s	d	£	s	d	£	s	d	£	s	d	£	s	d	£	s	d	£	s	d	£	s	d	£	s	d	£	s	d	£	s	d	£	s	d	£	s	d	

As regards the Grindery for the various departments, a store is kept for the various stocks of these articles, the stock for each room being kept distinct. Stock Books are kept, having a debit and credit account for each kind of article, and stores are only given out for written orders signed by the foreman of each room. At the end of each week a list of these orders is made out, and the total amount given out to each department sent in to the costing clerk.

Against this is placed the amounts receivable, arrived at by means of the Coupon Ticket. A rough Profit and Loss Account (Form 13) is thus obtained. To be quite accurate, of course, the stocks on hand in each room should be ascertained, but this is impossible; and the results will be approximately correct, because the stocks in each room should not vary materially.

Form 13.—

GRINDERY PROFIT AND LOSS SHEET.

For Week ending..............

	Machine Room	Lasting Room	Finishing Room
To Grindery sent up from Stores			
„ Grindery Receivable as per Coupons..			
„ Profit			
„ Loss			

These weekly records are summarised each month and again at Stock-takings

Occasionally the stocks of some of the articles in the store should be taken, and compared with the balances on their accounts in the Register of Stores Book.

The costings of the grindery for each room can also be checked in the bulk at each stocktaking, the Invoice Book supplying the purchases and the Coupon Tickets the amount receivable for materials used..

The whole of the materials in the costings have now therefore been dealt with. The checking of the costings of those raw materials such as skins for the uppers and materials for the bottoms, which in the working up afford scope for losses, is done in detail—as regards skins, at the time ; and at the time to some extent, and as far as possible, as regards bottom leather and the grindery for the various departments ; and a further checking is done also in the bulk at stocktakings when audited figures are available. The checking of the costings of these raw materials, on which, if worked up honestly with an average amount of skill, no loss whatever should be sustained, is done in the bulk at stocktakings. A Manufacturing Profit and Loss Account in respect of the materials worked up can therefore be easily prepared. All the necessary information is available— stocks, purchases, and the amount receivable for the whole of the materials worked up from the Coupon Tickets, which give particulars of the boots manufactured.

WAGES.

The Wages Book is kept in such a way that the operatives who perform the work of each class or series of operations costed for are classified together. That is to say, the clickers and other workers performing the operations covered by the labour operation of clicking in the costing are scheduled by themselves, the same method being followed as regards machinists, eyeletters, Press Room hands (who cut up the bottom stuff and socks), lasters, finishers, fitters-up, heelers, sewers, packers, managers, &c., so that by turning up the Summary of Wages each week the total wages paid to each class of operatives can be at once ascertained.

With this information and the coupons from each room a Wages Profit and Loss Account of each room is prepared every week, showing, on the one hand, the wages paid, and, on the other, the amount receivable in respect of the labour operations from the articles manufactured.

This gives only approximate results, because it takes no account of the stock of articles in each room, either at the commencement or the end of each week, upon each of which a certain amount of the total labour to be performed in each room may be expended. To ascertain these stocks by taking them is out of the question, but they should not vary considerably when business is maintained at a steady level. Should the weekly Profit and Loss Accounts show violent fluctuations, the aggregate figures for three or four weeks could be ascertained, and these would disclose more accurately the position of affairs.

When stocks are taken these weekly Profit and Loss Accounts are summarised, and the total result for the period ascertained.

Forms 14, 15, 16, 17, and 18 are rulings of books for ascertaining the wages receivable according to the coupons, together with other particulars for obtaining the necessary information as regards materials worked up and royalty for checking the costings in the bulk at stocktakings.

Form 14.— CLICKING ROOM.

Serial	Quantity	Boot No.	Labour Per doz. Prs.	Amount	Skins and Other Materials for Uppers	Amount
				£ s d	£ s d	£ s d
2,407	3 0	4,061	2/6	0 7 6	1 13 9	5 1 3

Form 15.—

MACHINE ROOM.

Serial	Quantity	Boot No.	Labour per doz. pairs	Amount	Eyelets per doz. pairs	Amount	Grindery per doz. pairs	Amount	Eyeletting	Amount
				£ s d		£ s d		£ s d		£ s d
2,407	3—0	4,061	3/3	0 9 9	9½d.	0 2 4½	3d.	0 0 9	2½d.	0 0 7½

Form 16.

FITTING-UP DEPARTMENT.

Serial	Quantity	Boot No.	Labour	Amount £ s d	Cutting Bottom Stuff	Amount £ s d	Bottom Stuff Socks	Amount £ s d
2,407	3—0	4,061	3d.	0 0 9	1/3	0 3 9	17/3	2 11 9

Form 17.—

LASTING ROOM.

Serial	Quantity	Boot No.	Labour	Amount £ s d	Grindery	Amount £ s d	Sewing and Cord	Amount £ s d	Royalty	Amount £ s d
2,407	3 0	4,061	3/9	0 11 3	7d.	0 1 9	5d.	0 1 3	3d.	0 0 9

Form 18.—

FINISHING ROOM.

Serial	Quantity	Boot No.	Labour	Amount £ s d	Grindery	Amount £ s d	Boxes	Amount £ s d	Packing Labour	Amount £ s d	Cost Price £ s d	Amount £ s d	Selling Price (each)	Amount £ s d
2,407	3 0	4,061	3/9	0 11 3	4d.	0 1 0	1/-	0 3 0	6d.	0 1 6	3 10 1	10 10 3	7/11	14 5 0

With reference to Form 18, relating to the Finishing Room, particular attention is directed to the last two columns. These provide for the cost price and selling price of the article. By means of the data supplied by these columns an account (Form 19) is prepared each week, showing the gross profit on goods manufactured; and also a further account (Form 20), showing approximately the value of the stock on hand at any given time. It will be noticed that the only estimated item in the latter is the amount of wages in respect of goods in process of manufacture, which, however, with the information available, should be almost correct. The stock as shown by this account should be checked by an account framed on the following lines (Form 21).

Form 22 is the Summary of the Wages Paid and Receivable for the week.

Form 19.—

MANUFACTURING PROFIT AND LOSS ACCOUNT for the month of January 1906.

1906		£	s	d	£	s	d	1906		£	s	d	£	s	d
Jan. 31	To Loss on Wages	56	0	0				Jan. 31	By Value of Goods manufactured, selling prices ..	10,000	0	0			
	" Manufacturing Profit for month	1,494	0	0	1,550	0	0		" Less prime cost of same..	8,500	0	0	1,500	0	0
									" Profits on cutting up skins	40	0	0			
									" Profits on consumption of Grinderies	10	0	0	50	0	0
					£1,550	0	0						£1,550	0	0

Form 20.—

STOCK ACCOUNTS.

RAW MATERIALS AND GOODS IN PROCESS.

1906		£	s	d	£	s	d	1906		£	s	d	£	s	d
Jan. 1	To Stock, Raw Materials ..	19,450	0	0				Jan. 31	By Goods Manufactured, prime cost	8,500	0	0			
	" Do. Goods in Process..	1,950	0	0	21,400	0	0		" Balance, being estimated Stock in hand	17,900	0	0	26,400	0	0
31	" Purchases				3,000	0	0								
	" Wages				2,000	0	0								
					£26,400	0	0						£26,400	0	0

FINISHED GOODS.

1906		£	s	d	£	s	d	1906		£	s	d	£	s	d
Jan. 1	To Stock				4,000	0	0	Jan. 31	By Goods sold				7,000	0	0
" 31	" Goods Manufactured				10,000	0	0		" Balance, being estimated Stock in hand ..				7,000	0	0
					£14,000	0	0						£14,000	0	0

SUMMARY.

1906		£	s	d	£	s	d	£	s	d
Jan. 31	To Stock, Raw Materials, &c.							17,900	0	0
	" Do. Finished Goods	£7,000	0	0						
	Less 15 % ..	1,050	0	0	5,950	0	0			
								23,850	0	0
	Add Estimated Wages on Goods in process							700	0	0
	Total Stock							£24,550	0	0

C 2

STOCK ACCOUNT.

Form 21.—

1906		£ s d	£ s d	1906		£ s d	£ s d
Jan. 1	To Stocks:—			Jan. 31	By Sales (*less* Returns) ...		7,000 0 0
	Raw Materials ...	19,450 0 0	—		*Less* Estimated Gross Profit 15 % ...		1,050 0 0
	Partly Manufactured ...	1,950 0 0	—				950 0 0
	Finished Goods ...	4,000 0 0					140 0 0
Jan. 31	„ Purchases		25,400 0 0		„ Estimated Stock ...		
	„ Wages		3,000 0 0				360 0 0
			2,000 0 0				
			£30,400 0 0				

Form 22.—

WAGES PROFIT AND LOSS SHEET for Week ending.................

	Clicking Room	Machine Room	Lasting Room	Finishing Room	Fitting up Department	Press Room	Packing	Foremen, &c.
To Wages Paid								
" Do. Receivable as per Coupons ..								
" Profit								
" Loss								

These Weekly records are summarised each month and again at Stocktakings.

As regards the above method of checking the costings of wages, probably the most accurate and satisfactory way to check the costings of wages is to check the costings of each order either in detail or in the bulk, but the clerical work and inconvenience such a system would involve render it impossible of application to this particular trade.

With further reference to the question of wages it must be borne in mind that the person responsible for the costings will be desirous—it is only in human nature that he should—of bringing out the cost as low as possible, and where there are different grades of labour receiving different rates of pay the tendency will be to cost on the lower grades, the consequence in all probability being that the workmen executing the lower grades cannot cope with all the work intended for them, and that the workmen on a higher scale of remuneration will have to come to their assistance.

Manufacturing Profit and Loss Accounts (Forms 23 and 24) of the whole of the prime cost can now be compiled, showing the sources of profits and losses. The purchases and wages are obtained from the books of account, and are the same as those in the audited Trading Account. The stocks are the same also. The coupons supply accurately the information necessary to ascertain the amounts receivable for every item in the prime cost on every article manufactured. The Manufacturing Trading, or Selling Account (Form 25) is then prepared, the debits to this account being the stock of manufactured goods at the commencement, the total amount receivable for materials and wages, and the credits being the sales, less returns, and the stock of manufactured goods at the end.

On preparing the usual Trading Account, the resultant profit will, of course, be the aggregate profits of the Manufacturing Account and the Manufacturing Trading, or Selling Account.

Form 23.—

		1st January 1906	31st December 1906				31st December 1906			
		Stocks	Wages	Purchases	Profit	Total	Amounts Receivable	Stock	Loss	Total
1	Skins and Materials for Uppers	£10,680	£..	£43,275	£775	£54,730	£44,905	£9,825	£..	£54,730
2	Sole Leather, Bottom Stuffs, and Heeling Wages	9,260	400	20,725	..	30,385	22,425	7,458	502	30,385
3	Cord, Boxes, and Sewing Wages	40	260	450	132	1,882	1,842	40	..	1,882
	Grinderies:—Machine Room									
4	Do. Lasting do.	30	..	350	..	380	325	28	27	380
5	Do. Lasting do.	40	..	800	..	840	758	42	40	840
6	Do. Finishing do.	50	..	500	..	550	433	46	71	550
7	Royalty	..	..	300	25	325	325	..	..	325
	Wages.									
8	Clickers	..	3,180	..	70	3,250	3,250	..	..	3,250
9	Machinists	..	3,725	..	500	4,225	4,225	..	..	4,225
10	Eyeletters	..	260	..	11	271	271	..	..	271
11	Press Room	..	1,700	..	..	1,700	1,625	..	75	1,700
12	Lasting	..	4,900	..	..	4,900	4,875	..	25	4,900
13	Finishing	..	5,000	..	..	5,000	4,875	..	125	5,000
14	Fitting Up	..	300	..	25	325	325	..	..	325
15	Packing and Treeing	..	600	..	50	650	650	..	..	650
		£20,100	£20,325	£67,400	£1,588	£109,413	£91,109	£17,439	£865	£109,413

Total Profits.. .. £1,588
Less Losses 865
　　　　　　　　£723

Form 24.—

MANUFACTURING ACCOUNT.

Date	Description	£ s d	£ s d	Date	Description	£ s d	£ s d
1906 Jan. 1	To Stock—			1906 Dec. 31	By Goods Manufactured	..	91,109 0 0
	Raw Materials	18,200 0 0			" Stock—		
	Partly Manufactured Goods ..	3,200 0 0			Raw Material	15,689 0 0	18,814 0 0
Dec. 31	" Purchases	..	21,400 0 0		Partly Manufactured Goods..	3,125 0 0	
	" Wages	..	67,400 0 0				
			20,325 0 0				£109,923 0 0
	" Profit	..	109,125 0 0				
			798 0 0		By Profit as above		
			£109,923 0 0		" Net Profit on Wages and Materials Worked up	798 0 0	
					" Difference : being increase in Stock of partly Manufactured Goods in Making Room, Lasting Room, Fitting Up Department, and Finishing Room	723 0 0	
						75 0 0	

Form 25.—

TRADING OR SELLING ACCOUNT.

		£	s	d				£	s	d
1906					1906					
Jan. 1	To Stock Finished Goods	4,000	0	0	Dec. 31	By Sales	123,000	0	0
Dec. 31	" Goods Manufactured	91,149	0	0	"	Stock Finished Goods	3,000	0	0
		95,109	0	0						
"	" Gross Profit .	30,851	0	0						
		£ 126,000	0	0			£ 126,000	0	0	

Oncost or Supplementary Cost.—

Oncost or supplementary cost is here used to denote the amount which is added to prime cost to cover expenses and standing charges. In the particular trade under consideration the amount to be added in respect of supplementary cost—and in most cases of profit also—is ascertained by way of a percentage, either on the prime cost or on the total amount of workmen's wages included therein. (The hourly rate and the machine rate are, in the writer's judgment, inapplicable to this industry.) Here is a further advantage to be gained from a checking of the items of prime cost.

Assuming that a manufacturer desires to make a gross profit of 25 per cent. upon his turnover to provide for supplementary cost, and he adopts the method of adding to prime cost, the percentage it would be necessary to add to secure the rate mentioned would be 33⅓ per cent. Now assuming that his estimated prime cost was below the actual cost by 5 per cent., the gross profit would work out at 21.25 per cent., and the amount earned for supplementary cost 1.25 per cent. less than if his prime cost had been accurate.

Again, assume that a manufacturer provides for supplementary cost by way of a percentage on the total of the items for wages in the prime cost, and that he adopts as his percentage the percentage of his expenses on the ' productive wages as shown in the Trading and Profit and Loss Accounts in respect of the preceding financial period, which percentage we will assume to be 50 per cent. Now if, unknown to him, as a matter of fact his costings for productive wages during that period were under-estimated, the percentage is less than it should be. Assuming the figures in the account to be Wages £10,000 and Expenses £5,000, and assuming that his estimates of the items of Wages in his costings were less than the actual cost by £2,500, the percentage of the expenses would then work out at 66.66 per cent.; or if the loss were regarded as an expense which he was unable to save, then the percentage would be 75 per cent.

PART II.

By means of the foregoing systems results are obtainable as to manufacturing. The results of trading or selling and the expenses incurred, together with financial matters, require to be dealt with.

Form 26 is a periodical statement for each calendar month, made up to the last day of each month. It cannot usually be prepared at once on the expiration of the month, as there may be several matters in abeyance involving a little delay in closing the books—such, for instance, as invoices for goods purchased, which for some reason or other have not been passed.

The upper portion of the form deals with the financial situation, and the lower provides, with the exception of the stocks, for all the details of a Trading and Profit and Loss Account, columns being given for the same items for the corresponding month of the previous year and for the totals to date in each case.

As regards the upper portion of the statement, the bank balance and cash and bills in hand can be ascertained from the Cash Book, Bill Book, and Petty Cash Book in a few minutes. The debtors and creditors can be obtained with very little difficulty, and in a short time, if the system of bookkeeeping provides for the Ledgers being self-balancing; otherwise they will have to be ascertained by the balances being abstracted in detail, which is sometimes a long business. Self-balancing Ledgers necessitate the analysis of cash received and paid away and of sales and purchases, if either are posted to other Ledgers than the Sales and Purchase Ledgers respectively. The same remark applies also to both Returns Books. Entries into Ledgers which do not fall to be passed through the subsidiary books mentioned must be journalised.

Form 26.—　DIRECTORS' MEETING................　.　....190....

FINANCIAL STATEMENT................190....

Corresponding period 190..		£ s d	£ s d		Corresponding period 190..		£ s d	£ s d
	To Creditors				By Debtors			
	" Bills				" Bank			
	" Bank				Bills			
	" Sundry				Cash and Cheques..			
					" Additions Capital Account..			
					Land and Buildings ..			
					Plant and Machinery ..			
					Power..			
					Tools..			
					Horses			
					Rolling Stock ..			
	" Surplus being excess of assets over liabilities exclusive of stock				" Other Capital Expenditure..			
					" Surplus being excess of liabilities over assets exclusive of stock			

Form 26—(continued).

COMPARISON OF SALES, PURCHASES, WAGES AND EXPENSES...........190.....

Totals to Date			
190..	190..	190..	190..
	£ s d	£ s d	

To Purchases ..
" Manufacturing Wages
" Carriage Inwards. ..
" Discounts ..
" Balance carried down..

To Gal Wages
Factory
Do. Counting
Rent, Rates and Taxes ..
Carriage Outwards
Travelling Expenses
Gal, Gas and Water
Advertising..
Repairs to Plant and Machinery..
Do. Tools..
Do. Mve Plant
Do. Rolling Stock
Postage & Stationery
Horse Keep..
Miscellaneous Expenses
Insurance ..
Patent Expenses
Legal do. ..
Auditors' Fees
Bank Charges
Bad Debts ..

Director's Fees
Ine Tax
Debenture Interest

By Sales (less Returns) ..
" Interest on Accounts ..

By Balance brought down ..

Orders on 190.. 190..
hand ..

Totals to Date			
190..	190..	190..	190..
	£ s d	£ s d	

Form 27.—   DEBTORS' ACCOUNT, 31st January 1905.

1905		£ s d		£ s d	1905			£ s d		£ s d
Jan. 1	To Debtors	: :		6,000 0 0	Jan. 31	By Cash received ...	: :			4,00 0 0
" 31	Sales (less Returns) ...	: :		5,000 0 0		" Bills do. ...	: :			500 0 0
						" Discount allowed	: :			225 0 0
						" Journal Entries	: :			35 0 0
										4,760 0 0
						" Balance carried down	:			6,240 0 0
				£11,000 0 0						£11,000 0 0
1905 Feb. 1	To Balance brought down	: :		6,240 0 0						

Form 28.—

CREDITORS' ACCOUNT, 31st January 1905.

1905		£ s d		£ s d	1905			£ s d		£ s d
Jan. 31	To Cash paid ...	: :		2,200 0 0	Jan. 1	By Creditors	: :			2,500 0 0
	" Discount received	: :		68 0 0	" 31	" Purchases (less Returns) ... (including Rent, Gas, Water, &c.)				2,000 0 0
	" Journal Entries	: :		35 0 0						
				2,303 0 0						
	" Balance carried down	:		2,197 0 0						
				£4,500 0 0						£4,500 0 0
					Feb. 1	By Balance brought down	:			2,197 0 0

In order to ascertain the debtors and creditors, accounts are raised similar to Forms 27 and 28. The balances at the commencement are, in both cases, those appearing on the Balance Sheet for the fiscal year just closed, which are, of course, the balances owing at the beginning of the new year. The sales and purchases are the amounts posted to the Nominal Ledger, less returns; the cash and bills and discounts are obtained from the Cash and Bill Books, and the Journal entries from the Journal. As regards discounts, an account is raised (Form 29) commencing on both sides with the reserves on the creditors and debtors. The discounts allowed and received during the month are posted from the Cash Book and Bill Book. The reserves on the balances at the end of the month are estimated in the most reliable way. The account is self-adjusting, so that in the event of the estimates being "out" they will in due course automatically correct themselves.

As regards the lower portion of the account, this, so far as the trading and profit and loss items are concerned, is an abstract of the Nominal and Private Ledgers. The manufacturing gross profit is shown, and also the percentage of same on selling prices of goods manufactured. If the goods are made for orders it is safe to assume that the same percentage of gross profit is being made on the sales, unless there are serious fluctuations in the prices of raw materials; so that there has been ascertained what gross profit is being earned to meet expenses incurred and the net profit on manufacturing and on selling. It may be that some of the sales are from goods in stock at the commencement of the period. If considered desirable, such sales can be earmarked, and the gross profit arrived at by ascertaining the amount at which they were taken at stocktaking.

A valuable check on the accuracy of the bookkeeping is provided by the item of "Surplus" in the Financial Statement, as this figure should fluctuate exactly by the amount of the

Form 29.—

DISCOUNT ACCOUNT, January 1905.

		£ s d	£ s d			£ s d	£ s d
1905 Jan. 31	To Discount reserved on Debtors	: :	300 0 0	1905 Jan. 1	By Discount reserved on Creditors	: :	75 0 0
"	" Do. All val ..	: :	225 0 0	" 31	" Do. 1 wl ..	: :	68 0 0
"	" Do. reserved on Creditors	: :			" Do. reserved on Debtors	: :	311 0 0
	£2,197 carried down ..	: :	66 0 0		" £40 carried wn	: :	
					" Bal a, being less in respect of Discounts for the month	: :	137 0 0
			£591 0 0				£591 0 0
Feb. 1	To Reserve on Debtors brought down	: :	311 0 0	Feb. 1	By Reserve on Creditors brought down	: :	66 0 0

difference between the debit and credit sides of the lower portion of the form.

If considered desirable the stocks can be included, the stock to start with being the stock on hand at the commencement of the financial period, and the stock at the end being the estimated stock ascertained according to the method illustrated by Form 20 in Part I.

Fluctuations of Floating Capital.—

At the end of each financial period an account should be prepared showing these fluctuations.

Form 30 is a Balance Sheet on the 1st January 1904, the commencement of the period. A simple instance is chosen to illustrate the principle. The working capital is £24,000, consisting of—

Stock	£10,000
Book Debts	6,000
Bills	4,000
Cash	10,000
	30,000
Less Liabilities	6,000
	£24,000

Form 31 is a Balance Sheet as at the end of the year 31st December 1904. The working capital is as follows:—

Stock	£12,000
Book Debts	4,500
Bills	3,000
Cash	10,500
	30,000
Less Liabilities	5,500
	£24,500

Form 30.—

BALANCE SHEET, 1st January 1904.

Liabilities.	£	s	d	Assets.	£	s	d
To Capital	30,000	0	0	By Plant and Machinery	6,000	0	0
" Creditors	6,000	0	0	" Stock	10,000	0	0
				" Book Debts	6,000	0	0
				" Bills	4,000	0	0
				" Cash	10,000	0	0
	£36,000	0	0		£36,000	0	0

Form 31.—

BALANCE SHEET, 31st December 1904.

Liabilities.	£	s	d	£	s	d	Assets.	£	s	d	£	s	d
To Capital				30,000	0	0	By Plant and Machinery as at 1st January 1904	6,000	0	0			
" Creditors				5,500	0	0	" Additions since	1,000	0	0			
" Reserve Fund				500	0	0		7,000	0	0			
" Profit and Loss—							Less Depreciation	700	0	0	6,300	0	0
Profit for the year	3,800	0	0				" Stock				12,000	0	0
Less Dividends	3,500	0	0	300	0	0	" Book Debts				4,500	0	0
							" Bills				3,000	0	0
							" Cash				10,500	0	0
				£36,300	0	0					£36,300	0	0

The additional amount of £500 is made up as follows:—

Reserve Fund		£500
Profits retained		300
		800
Less net amount of Expenditure on Plant and Machinery ..		300
		£500

Form 32 is a Balance Sheet as at the end of the year following 31st December 1905. During the year debentures amounting in the aggregate to £10,000 have been issued and subscribed, and the proceeds thereof utilised for the purposes of purchasing freehold land and erecting buildings thereon. Trustees for the debenture-holders have been appointed under a trust deed, which provides for the payment to them annually of the sum of £500 for the purpose of redeeming the debentures.

The working capital is as follows:—

Stock			£11,000
Book Debts			7,000
Bills			1,000
Cash			8,650
			27,650
Less Trade Liabilities	£4,500		
„ Amount owing for Debenture Interest	250		
			4,750
			£22,900

On the original amount of working capital of £24,000 there is a diminution of £1,100, made up as follows:—

Net amount of expenditure on Machinery ..		£1,300
Cash utilised for redemption of Debentures ..		500
		1,800
Less Reserve Fund	£500	
„ Profits retained	200	
		700
		£1,100

Form 32.—

BALANCE SHEET, 31st December 1905.

Liabilities.	£ s d	£ s d		Assets.	£ s d	£ s d
To Capital		30,000 0 0		By Freehold Property		10,000 0 0
" Debentures Issued and Subscribed	10,000 0 0			" Plant and Machinery as at 31st December 1904	6,300 0 0	
Less Amount Redeemed	500 0 0			Additions since	1,500 0 0	
	9,500 0 0				7,800 0 0	
Add Interest accrued	250 0 0	9,750 0 0		Less Depreciation	500 0 0	7,300 0 0
" Creditors		4,500 0 0		" Stock		11,000 0 0
" Reserve Fund		500 0 0		" Book Debts		7,000 0 0
" Profit and Loss Account:—				" Bills		1,000 0 0
Amount brought forward from 31st December 1904	300 0 0			" Cash		8,650 0 0
Profit for the year	2,000 0 0					
	2,300 0 0					
Less Dividends	2,100 0 0	200 0 0				
		£44,950 0 0				£44,950 0 0

The account brings out clearly the position of affairs and how it is produced. It is obvious that if the diminution is continued at this rate a serious position will soon be developed.

Monthly Budget.—

Form 33 illustrates the lines on which this should be framed. This shows the estimated funds available for the requirements of the next month, the actual figures of the corresponding month of the previous year, and also the total figures to date. This information is, of course, extremely useful and valuable.

Form 3. — MONTHLY BUDGET for the Month of....... ...190...

Totals to Date		190..	190..	Totals to Date	190..	190..
190..	90 ..	£ s d	£ s d		£ s d	£ s d

To Balance at Bank
   " Cash and Cheques on hand
   " Bills on hand
   " Receipts (estimated 190)—
      Cash..
      Bills..
      Sundry

By Balance due to Bank (estimated)
   " Expenditure 190)—
   For Goods..
    " Wages..
    " Expenses
    " Factors' Fees
    " Debenture Interest..
    " Interim dvds..

INDEX.

		PAGE
Analysis of Cash	...	· 37
Ascertainment of Items of Cost	...	7
Average Cost	...	7
Balance Sheets		... 44, 46
Book, Invoice		... 20
Boot, Description of	...	6
Bottom Filling	... ...	7
,, Leather	... ...	17
,, ,, Profit and Loss Account		18
,, ,, Record of Cutting Book		17
,, ,, Stock Book	...	10
,, Stuff Costing Sheet		10
Bottoms	... ...	10
,, Coupons for	...	19
Boxes, Checking Costings of		19
Bungs	... ...	1
Capital, Fluctuations of Floating	... ...	43, 44, 45, 46
,, Working	...	... 43
Cash, Analysis of	...	37
Checking Cost of each Order		32
,, Costings	...	... 3
,, Bottom Stuff	...	... 17, 19
,, Cord and Boxes	...	... 19
,, Grinderies		... 21, 22
,, Royalty...		... 19
,, Uppers ...		... 19
,, ,, Wages ...	...	23, 24, 25, 26
Classes of Labour Operations		... 3
Clickers	... ...	7
Clicking Room Description Book	...	12
Comparative Monthly Financial Statement	...	37

	PAGE
Consecutive Numbers (orders) ...	12
Cord	12
Cost, Ascertainment of Items of ...	7
„ Average	7
„ Items of	6, 7
„ Prices and Selling Prices ...	27
Costing Book	3
„ Clerk 12, 21	
„ Description of Book	6
„ Explanation of Specimen of ...	5, 6
„ of Heels	10
„ „ Soles	5
„ Sheet (Bottom Stuff) ·	10
„ „ (Uppers) ...	8, 9
„ Specimen of ...	4
Costings, Business of ...	3
„ Checking of ...	3
„ Points to bear in mind ...	2
„ Principles to be observed	2
Coupon Ticket 11, 12	
Coupons 12, 32	
„ for Bottoms	19
„ „ Grinderies 21, 22	
„ „ Wages	22
Creditors, How to obtain ...	41
Debtors, How to obtain ...	41
Department, Fitting up	17
„ „ (Surprise Visits)	19
Departments of Productive Labour ...	3, 5
Description Book for Clicking Room	12
„ of Boot in Costing ...	6
„ Costing Sheet (Uppers)	8
„ Goods in Process Book	12
„ Record of Cuttings Book	14
„ Skin Stock Book ...	16
„ Use of Coupon Ticket	12

	PAGE
Description of Weekly Summary of Profits and Losses, Cutting up Materials	16
Discounts	41
Disposal of Rooms	5
Explanation of Specimen Costing ...	5, 6
Eyelets	3
„ Profit and Loss Account ...	19
Facings, Profit and Loss Account	19
Financial Statement, Monthly Comparative	37
Filling, Bottom	7
Fitting ...	6
Fitting-up Department	17
Fluctuations of Floating Capital	43, 44, 45, 46
Forms—	

Balance Sheets ...	Form	30, 31	44
	„	32	46
Checking Cost of Wages—			
Clicking Room ...	„	14	23
Finishing „ ...	„	18	26
Fitting-up Department ...	„	16	25
Lasting Room ...	„	17	26
Machine „ ...	„	15	24
Costing Sheet, Bottom Stuff ...		4	10
„ „ Uppers	„	2, 3	8, 9
Coupon Ticket ...		5	11
Creditors	„	28	40
Cutting-up Materials ...		9	16
Debtors	„	27	40
Discounts	„	29	42
Goods in Process Book ...		7	14
Grindery Profit and Loss Account	„	13	21
Invoice Book	„	12	20
Manufacturing Profit and Loss Account	„	19	28
„ Trading or Selling Account	„	25	35
Monthly Comparative Financial Statement	„	26	38, 39

                                                                  PAGE
Forms—

    Prime Cost, Manufacturing, Profit and
       Loss Account   ...   .   Form 23, 24   33, 34
       Profit and Loss Account, Bottom Leather ,,   11   18
       ,,   ,,   ,, Sheet, Wages ...   ,,   22   31
       Record of Cuttings Book   8   15
       Skin Stock Book   ...   ,,   10   16
       Specimen Costing   ...   1   4
       Stock Accounts   ...   ,,   20, 21   29, 30
       Work Ticket   6   13

Goods in Process Book 7, 12
Grinderies—
    Checking Costs of 21, 22
    Coupon 21, 22
    Profit and Loss Account   13, 21, 22
    Stock Book   21
Gross Profit 27, 41

Half Lifting   ...   10
Heels   10

Insoles   ...   10
Invoice Book 12, 20
Items of Cost   ...   6, 7

Labour, Departments of Productive ...   3, 5
    ,,   Operations, Classes of   ...   3
Last 5, 6
Ledgers, Self-Balancing   ...   37
Lifts   ...   10
Lines, Running-in   .   8
Linings 9, 19
Lots of Skins, Profits and Losses on   17

Management per cent.   ...   7
Manufacturing Prime Costs   ...   32
    ..   Profit and Loss Account   28
        Trading or Selling Account   ...   32

PAGE

Middles or Middle Sole 10
Moulds for Heels 10

Offal ... 8
Oncost or Supplementary Cost 36
Operations, Classes of Labour ... 3
Order Book ... 12
Orders, Consecutive Number 12
   ,,   Serial Number ... 12
Outsoles 10

Packing Room 5
Price Selling 3
Productive Labour, Departments of ... 3, 5
Profit and Loss Account—
   Bottom Leather 17, 18
   Grinderies 13, 21
   Linings, Facings, Top Bands. Eyelets, Tongues, &c. ... 19
   Manufacturing 28
   Prime Cost 32
   Wages 22
   Weights Costing Sheet (Uppers) ... 9
Profit, Gross 27
Profits and Losses, Weekly Summary, Materials 16
   ,,   ,,   ,,   Lots of Skins 17
Puffs ... 7

Record of Cuttings Book (Bottoms) 17
   ,,   ,,   ,,   (Uppers) ... 14, 15, 18
Room, Packing 5
   ..   Skin 5
   ,,   Stock 5
Rooms, Disposal of ... 5
Royalty, Checking Costings of ... 9
Running-in Lines ... 8

Scrap 9
Seat Lifts ... 10
Self-Balancing Ledgers 37

	PAGE
Selling Price ...	3
Serial Numbers (Orders) ...	12
Sewing ...	7
Shanking ...	7
Sheet Costing (Uppers) ...	8, 9
Skin Room ...	5
,, Stock Book	10, 16, 17
Skins ...	7, 17
,, Variability of	7, 9
Soles, Costing of	5
Specimen Costing	4, 5, 6
Standard Oil Trust	1
Stiffner ...	0
Stock Accounts	29, 30
,, Boot Legs, &c. ...	8
,, Room ...	5
Stocks ...	43
,, of Stores ...	21
,, on Hand, Approximate	27
Stores, Grindery ...	21
Summary of Profits and Losses ...	16
Supplementary Cost ...	36
Surplus ...	41
Surprise Visits ...	16
Taking Stocks of Shares ...	21
Ticket Coupon ...	11
,, Work ...	11
Tongues ...	8, 19
Topbands ...	9, 19
Top Pieces ...	10
Trading Manufacturing or Selling Account ...	32
Uppers, Costing Sheet ...	8, 9
,, Checking Costings	19
Variability of Skins ...	7, 9
Visits, Surprise...	19

		PAGE
Wages		... 22, 32
,, Book		... 22
,, Checking Costs of ...	...	23, 24, 25, 26
,, Coupon ...		... 22
,, Profit and Loss Account	...	22
,, ,, ,, ,, Sheet		31
,, Summary ...		22
Work Ticket ...		11
Working Capital		43

	Price Post Free
Bankruptcy. Trustee's Estate Book. (Dicksee) each 4/4; doz.	40/-
Bookkeeping, Antiquity of. (Heaps)	1/1
,, **Elementary.** (Day)	1/2
Elements of. (Streeter)	1/9
,, **Exercises.** (Dicksee)	3/9
,, **for Accountant Students.** (Dicksee) (5th Edition)	10/6
,, **Company Secretaries.** (Dicksee) (4th Edition)	5/4
,, **Executors and Trustees.** (Hawkins)	3/9
,, **Publishers.** (Allen)	2/9
,, **Retail Traders.** (Findlay) ...	3/3
, ,, **Record Book.** (Findlay)	4/4
,, **Solicitors.** (Hodsoll)	3/9
,, **Technical Classes and Schools.** (Clarke)	2/9
,, **Principles of.** (Carlill)	3/6
Boot and Shoe Costings. (Headly)	2/9
Brewers' and Bottlers' Accounts. (Lanham) ...	10/6
Brickmakers' Accounts. (Fox)	3/9
Builders' Accounts. (Walbank) (2nd Edition) ...	3/9
Building Societies' Accounts. (Grant-Smith) ...	3/9
,, **Society Table and Loan Calculations.** (Johnson.)	1/1
Chartered Accountants' Charges. (Pixley) (3rd Edition)	10/6
Companies Act, 1900. (Reid)	1/1
,, ,, ,, **Duties of Auditors under**	1/1
,, ,, **1907.** (Blount Lean)	1/1
Company Secretary. (Fox) (5th Edition) ...	25/-
,, **Winding-up Time Table**	-/7
Compendium, Accountant's. (Dawson) (3rd Edition in the press)	
Compensation for Man and Maid. (Wihl) ...	2/3
Co-operative Societies' Accounts. (Sugden) ...	5/4
Cost Accounts (Hawkins)	5/4
,, ,, **for Small Manufacturers.** (Jenkinson)	1/1
,, ,, **Multiple.** (Garry)	3/9
,, ,, **of an Engineer and Ironfounder.** (Best)	2/9
,, ,, **Process.** (Garry)	5/4
,, ,, **Single.** (Mitchell)	5/4
,, ,, **Terminal.** (Nesbit)	3/9
Cotton Spinners' Accounts. (Moss)	5/4
Dairy Accounts. (Rowland)	3/9
Deeds of Arrangement. (Davies)	8/-
Depreciation, Reserves, and Reserve Funds. (Dicksee)	3/9

	Price Post Free
Depreciation Tables. (Dicksee)	1/2
Drapers' Accounts. (Richardson)	3/9
Early Stages of Preparation for the Accountancy Papers of the Intermediate. (Cutforth) ...	2/9
Electric Lighting Accounts. (Johnson)	5/4
Engineers' and Shipbuilders' Accounts. (Burton)	3/9
Errors in Balancing. (2nd Edition)...	1/2
Examination Guide, Intermediate. (Nixon) ...	3/9
,, ,, **Final.** (Nixon)	5/4
,, **Papers (Questions & Answers)** May and November in each year, each ...	2/8
Examinations, A Month before the (Cutforth)...	1/6
,, **Chartered Accountants', How to Prepare for.** (Carlill) ...	1/7
Executorship Accounts. (Caldicott) (3rd Edition)	3/9
,, **Accounts, Student's Guide to.** (With 1907 Supplement) (Carter) ...	5/4
,, **Accounts.** (Whinney) (2nd Edition)	7/6
Factory Accounts. (Garcke & Fells) (5th Edition)	7/6
Fishing Industry Accounts. (Williamson) ...	3/9
Forms of Accounts. (Johnston)	2/9
Fraud in Accounts	3/9
Friendly Societies' Accounts. (Furnival Jones)...	5/4
Gas Accounts (2nd Edition)...	5/3
Goodwill and its Treatment in Accounts. (Dicksee & Tillyard) (3rd Edition)	5/6
Grain, Hay, &c., Accounts. (Johnson)	3/9
Grocers' Bookkeeping. (Jenkinson)	1/2
Hire-Purchase Wagon Trade, &c., Bookkeeping and Accounts for. (Johnson)	1/8
Hotel Accounts. (Dicksee)	3/9
How to Read a Balance Sheet. (Pixley) ...	-/7
Income Tax on Earnings. (Isaacs)	-/7
,, ,, **Practice, Guide to.** (Murray & Carter) (4th Edition)	10/-
,, ,, **with Special Reference to Recent Legislation** (Carter)	5/-
Insurance Companies' Accounts. (Tyler)... ...	10/6
Jewellers' Accounts. (Allen Edwards)	5/4
Laundry Accounts. (Livesey)	3/9
Legal Decisions Affecting Auditors, a Summary of. (Cocke)	1/1
Lexicon for Trustees in Bankruptcy, &c. Bound Boards. (Dawson)	3/9
Limited Partnership Act 1907 (Davies)	1/7½
List of Members. (Institute of Chartered Accountants)	2/3
Local Authorities' Accounts, Audit and Organisation of. (Collins)	12/6
Medical Practitioners' Accounts. (May)... ...	3/9
Metric System. (Streeter)	1/1

	Price Post Free
Mineral Water Manufacturers' Accounts. (Lund & Richardson) ...	3/9
Multiple Cost Accounts. (Garry) ...	3/9
,, **Shop Accounts.** (Hazelip) ...	3/9
Municipal Accounts. (Allcock) ...	10/6
,, **Finance for Students** ...	2/9
,, **Internal Audit.** (Collins) ...	3/9
,, **Rating.** (Pearce) ...	5/4
Newspaper Accounts. (Norton & Feasey) ...	10/-
Parliamentary Companies. (Keen) ...	1/1
Partnership Accounts. (Child) (4th Edition) ...	2/9
Pawnbrokers' Accounts. (Thornton & May) ...	3/9
Personal and Domestic Accounts. (Ibotson) ...	1/2
Polytechnic Accounts. (Calder Marshall) ...	3/9
Printers' Accounts. (Lakin-Smith) ...	3/9
Professional Accountants. (Worthington) ...	2/9
Publishers' Accounts. (Allen) ...	2/9
Quarry Accounts. (Ibotson) ...	3/9
Rating, Municipal. (Pearce) ...	5/4
Retail Traders, Account Book for. (Day) ...	5/4
Shipping Accounts. (Daly) ...	3/9
Shopkeepers' Accounts. (Quin) (2nd Edition) ...	2/9
Solicitors' Accounts. (Dicksee) ...	3/9
Some Legal Terms ...	1/1
Stamp Duties and Receipts, Handbook to. (Lakin-Smith) ...	2/9
Stockbrokers' Accounts. (Callaway) ...	3/9
Student's Guide to Accountancy. (2nd Edition)	2/9
Table A. [Revised] ...	-/7
Terminal Cost Accounts. (Nesbit) ...	3/9
Theatre Accounts. (Chantrey) ...	3/9
Timber Merchants' Accounts. (Smith) ...	3/9
Tramway Bookkeeping and Accounts. (McColl) with Supplement ...	12/6
Tramway Bookkeeping and Accounts Simplified. (The supplement to above work) (McColl) separately	2/9
Trial Balance Book, "Handy" each -/7; doz.	5/4
Trustees, Chart of the Rights and Duties of. (Willson)	1/3
,, **Liquidators, and Receivers, Accounts of.** (Dawson) ...	3/9
,, **Liquidators, and Receivers, Law of** (Willson) (2nd Edition) ...	10/-
Underwriters' Accounts. (Spicer & Pegler) ...	3/9
Urban District Councils' Accounts. (Eckersley)	5/4
Vade-Mecum, Accountant's and Bookkeeper's. (Whatley) ...	7/6
Van de Linde's Bookkeeping. (2nd Edition) ...	7/6
Water Companies' Accounts. (Key) ...	3/9
Wine and Spirit Merchants' Accounts. (Sabin) ...	5/4
Woollen, &c., Accounts. (Mackie) ...	3/9

DEPRECIATION, RESERVES, AND RESERVE FUNDS. Price 3s. 6d. net. 80 pages. By LAWRENCE R. DICKSEE, M.Com., F.C.A.

This Work—which is Vol. XXVI. of "THE ACCOUNTANTS' LIBRARY" series— deals fully and impartially with the most Debatable and Important Subjects in connection with Accounts.

It is divided into Twelve Chapters, with a Complete Index, and is the most Exhaustive Work upon the subject that has yet been issued.

EARLY STAGES of PREPARATION for the ACCOUNTANCY PAPERS of the INTERMEDIATE. By A. E. CUTFORTH, A.C.A. Price 2s. 6d. net.

ELECTRIC LIGHTING ACCOUNTS. Price 5s. net. Over 140 pages. By GEORGE JOHNSON, F.S.S., F.C.I.S.

This Work deals very fully with the Accounts of Electric Lighting Companies. It is divided into 18 Chapters, and contains a set of *pro formâ* transactions, with a complete index.

EXAMINATION GUIDES.—INTERMEDIATE AND FINAL. Price 3s. 6d. and 5s. net respectively. By JOHN G. NIXON, Junr., A.C.A.

These Books have been compiled in order to provide Accountant Students with a series of the Questions actually set at the Examinations of the Institute.

EXECUTORS AND TRUSTEES, BOOKKEEPING FOR. By L. WHITTEM HAWKINS, A.C.A. 84 pages. Price 3s. 6d. net. Contains full and explicit directions for keeping the Books and preparing the Accounts of Trust Estates, supplemented by a Specimen Set of Books and Examples of Statements of Account. The Specimen Set of Books is specially bound, so that it can be examined side by side with the text relating to it.

EXECUTORSHIP ACCOUNTS. Third Edition. (2nd Thousand). Price 3s. 6d. net. Revised under the FINANCE ACT and brought up to date. By O. H. CALDICOTT, F.C.A. Containing a COMPLETE SET of TRUST ACCOUNTS with explanatory text.

EXECUTORSHIP ACCOUNTS, STUDENT'S GUIDE TO, with 1907 Supplement. 264 pages. Price 5s. net. By ROGER N. CARTER, F.C.A. (Senior Honours Institute Examination, June 1893), Joint Author with Mr. Adam Murray, F.C.A., of "A Guide to Income-Tax Practice."

EXECUTORSHIP LAW AND ACCOUNTS. Second Edition. Price 7s. 6d. Revised and brought up to date by FREDERICK WHINNEY, Junr., B.A., Barrister-at-Law, assisted by ARTHUR P. VAN NECK, M.A., Barrister-at-Law.

Containing an Epitome of a Will and a Set of Executorship Accounts. By ARTHUR F. WHINNEY, F.C.A.

FRAUD IN ACCOUNTS. Price 3s. 6d. This Work deals with the methods of circumventing Frauds on the part of both Employees and Directors, and shows how they may be detected at an early date.

GAS ACCOUNTS (Vol. VII. of "THE ACCOUNTANTS' LIBRARY.") Price 5s. net.

This Work—which comprises 128 pages—deals fully with the Accounts of all classes of Gas undertakings. It contains an Introduction and Seven Chapters, and a Full Index is appended.

GOODWILL. Third Edition. Revised and Enlarged. By LAWRENCE R. DICKSEE, M.Com., F.C.A. Price 5s. 6d. net.

Although issued as the *Third Edition* of Professor Dicksee's well-known "GOODWILL," first published in 1897, this Volume has been so re-written and enlarged as to be for all practical purposes *an entirely New and Original Work of the Greatest Value to Accountants, Accountant Students, and Business Men.*

INCOME-TAX PRACTICE, A GUIDE TO. Fourth Edition. Revised and Enlarged. Price 10s. net. By ADAM MURRAY and ROGER N. CARTER, Chartered Accountants, Manchester.

Containing a Summary of the various Enactments relating to Income-Tax; Instructions as to the preparation of Returns for Assessment and Accounts in support of Appeals on the ground of over-assessment; also for claiming Exemption and Abatement; and a concise popular digest of the principal legal decisions on the construction of the Acts.

JEWELLERS', SILVERSMITHS', & KINDRED TRADERS' ACCOUNTS 170 pages. Price 5s. net. By ALLEN EDWARDS.

This Work deals fully with the Accounts of Manufacturing, Wholesale, and Retail Jewellers, and is clearly and concisely illustrated by upwards of fifty Forms, specially drawn up for the Work.

LIMITED PARTNERSHIPS ACT, 1907, containing the Full Act, Rules, and Forms. 70 pages. Demy 8vo. Price 1s. 7d. post free. By DAVID PRICE DAVIES, F.S.A.A.

Deals fully with the Limited Partnerships Act, 1907; Some Continental and other Provisions relating to Limited Partnerships; The Relation between the Partnership Act, 1890, and the Limited Partnerships Act, 1907. It contains the Rules, the full text of the Limited Partnerships Act, 1907, and of the Partnership Act, 1890, with an Index.

LOCAL AUTHORITIES' ACCOUNTS, THE ORGANISATION AND AUDIT OF. By ARTHUR COLLINS, F.S.A.A. Over 450 pages. Price 12s. 6d. net.

The only complete treatise on a subject now engaging the attention of Government Departments, all Local Authorities (members and officials), and every Professional Accountant. Incorporates the Recommendations of the Departmental Committee on Municipal Accounts. An exposition of up-to-date methods of financial control, collated from the most efficient systems in use in the leading local authorities of the Kingdom. The whole of the present day systems of Audit reviewed, analysed, and compared.

MONTH BEFORE THE EXAMINATION, THE. By ARTHUR E. CUTFORTH, A.C.A. Price 1s. 6d. net.

This little book has been compiled for the convenience of Examination Candidates. In it the author has collected in handy form those portions of each subject which are considered most difficult to retain in the memory for any length of time. An exception has been made in the case of the "Rights and Duties of Liquidators, Trustees, and Receivers," as condensed text-books thereon are in constant use by every Candidate during the whole course of his preparation.

MUNICIPAL ACCOUNTS. Price 10s. 6d. net. 200 pages. By JOHN ALLCOCK.

In this Volume the entire system of Bookkeeping and checking of Municipal Accounts is dealt with, and facsimiles of all Books and Forms recommended are given.

MUNICIPAL FINANCE FOR STUDENTS. Price 2s. 6d. net.

This Work on the most important features in Local Government Finance has been published in pursuance of an effort to respond to the demand for works on Municipal Accountancy at a reasonable price suitable for Students preparing for Examinations.

MUNICIPAL INTERNAL AUDIT, A. Price 3s. 6d. net. 150 pages. By ARTHUR COLLINS.

This Work will be found to be of especial importance to Municipal Financial Officers, Auditors of Municipal Accounts, Students of Municipal Accountancy, and members of the Profession engaged in the keeping and Audit of Municipal Accounts.

MUNICIPAL RATING AND THE COLLECTION OF RATES. By A. JAMES PEARCE, A.C.A. 96 pages. Price 5s. net.

PARTNERSHIP ACCOUNTS. Fourth Edition. Price 2s. 6d. net. By PERCY CHILD, A.C.A.

The points dealt with in this work are—
The Parole Agreement—The Agreement by Deed—The Partnership Act and the Deed—The Opening of Partnership Accounts—The Partnership Transactions—The Dissolution—An explanation of Partnership terms—The decision in *Garner v. Murray.*

PERSONAL AND DOMESTIC ACCOUNTS. By
J. G. P. IBOTSON, A.C.A. 56 pages. Cloth. Price 1s. net.

PUBLISHERS' ACCOUNTS. Price 2s. 6d. By C. E. ALLEN.
This Book deals fully with the nature and practice of the Publishing Business, the method of recording the Transactions, and the points to be noticed in connection with the Audit and the Treatment of Copyright.

RIGHTS AND DUTIES OF TRUSTEES, LIQUIDATORS, AND RECEIVERS, CHART OF THE. Price 1s. net. By W. R.
WILLSON, B.A., Barrister-at-Law.
This Chart, which gives at a glance a bird's-eye view of the leading features of the offices of Trust_____ _____ ____
designed for th
introduction to

SOLICIT

This Volum
practices. T
alternative me
work contains
method of kee

STAMP
E
The Book co
fees payable u
the rates and

STOCKB

The unique
Exchange is f
Exchange Wo

STUDEN

This Work
profession, and
Student the me

TRAMW
Supple
12s. 6d. ne
This Work i
in the Glasgo
service to Tra
fully described
In the Supple
tramway acco
results with les
first part of th

TRUSTE
AND
Revised a
of the Mid
on those
analyticall
Society of
the offices

WATER

This Work—
deals at length
necessary book
and extracts fr

AUTH_____ _____ _____ ___ ___LISHED.

CPSIA information can be obtained
at www.ICGtesting.com
Printed in the USA
BVHW04*1112100918
527043BV00010B/468/P